The Museum of Light

Other books by the author:

The Museum of Improvisation (Wild Honey Press, 2002)
A Hawk into Everywhere [with Roselle Angwin] (Stride, 2001)
Home All Along (Chrysalis Poetry, 1999)
Sirens Singing In The Grey Morning (Chrysalis Poetry Pamphlets, 1998)
Frosted Light: fourteen sequences, 1978-1988
(University of Salzburg, 1996)
The Giving of Flowers (Headland, 1994)
Timbers Across The Sun (University of Salzburg Press, 1993)
Between Dark Dreams (Acumen Books, 1992)
Pitched At Silence (The Tenorman Press, 1991)

The Museum of Light

Rupert M. Loydell

Rupert M. Loydell

Exeter Text

Arc
PUBLICATIONS

2003

Published by Arc Publications
Nanholme Mill, Shaw Wood Road
Todmorden, Lancs. OL14 6DA

Design by Tony Ward
Printed by Antony Rowe Ltd
Eastbourne, East Sussex

ISBN 1 900072 58 0

Acknowledgments:
Some of these poems first appeared in *Entropy*,
Epoch, *Fire*, *The Lucid Stone* (USA), *Salt* (Aus-
tralia), *Scratch*, *Southfields*, and *Third Way* maga-
zines. 'Polaroid Epiphanies', 'Instructions For The
Journey' and 'The Standing Still Of The Present
Time' were published in *World Of Wonder* (Od-
yssey Poets, 1997). 'Instructions For The Jour-
ney', 'Further Instructions For The Journey' and
'Final Instructions For The Journey' were pub-
lished in *Slipping Into The Palace Unnoticed*
(Trombone Press, 1997). Three poems from
'Background Noise' were published as a booklet
which was given away at The Living Room on 26
October 1997. 'Background Noise 3' was pub-
lished as a booklet which was given away at The
Living Room during February 1998. 'Background
Noise', 'Background Noise 2', and Background
Noise 3' were published as *Background Noise I-
III* by tel-let, Charleston, Illinois, USA in January
1999.

Cover photo by Sue Loydell

The Publishers acknowledge financial assistance
from Yorkshire Arts Board

CONTENTS

For Sue and Natasha

'Thinking is trying to think of the unthinkable:
thinking the thinkable is not worth the effort.
Painting is trying to paint what you cannot paint and
writing is writing what you cannot know before you
have written: it is preknowing and not knowing,
blindly, with words. It occurs at the point where light
and darkness meet.'
– Hélène Cixous

'While looking for the light, you may suddenly
be devoured by the darkness and find the true light.'
– Jack Kerouac, *The Scripture of the Golden Eternity*

BACKGROUND NOISE

My work is governed by secret rules
I am reluctant to give away.
Emotional responses are not enough,

the whole business is intense and obsessive –
compressing social indignation into memorable form
is a necessity for an artist who can't quite focus.

I pull bits of loveliness away from experience
(as if narrative wasn't cumbersome enough)
and reshuffle the uncertainties of life.

Elements of opposition are always present:
a fine eye for urban exotica and signs of modernity,
the uninflected quality of the readymade.

Signs and symbols pursue me. I am
not accorded the right to stare into the crowd
despite the smell of panic in the air.

Nowhere do we have need of these expressions.
This is a metaphoric and literal scavenging –
the secondary information acts as a periphery.

Like a gunshot, the silence is punctuated.
A melancholic ambience fills the space.
I just saw the world going by, trying to raise money.

These are nothing but facts – and phenomena:
a generation of stereotypes, an intriguing collage;
imaginative patterning, inevitable motifs,

a delicious whisper from the jukebox...
Playful laments for lost love –
a little awkward, but almost hummable.

•

We sit on the beach
drying slowly in the warm night air,
crying for the whole world.

Hoping for quick success,
a deep sense of mourning
appealingly packaged.

Such a pretty day here.
I'm sure you must have
an eye on what will sell?

Sincere discussions of loyalty
and betrayal ensue.
All could be forgiven.

Enter the elusive author.
He has shown many faces
to the public during his career,

developed a nasty habit of
blaming everyone else
when questions are raised.

•

Which way is up?
Which way is out?
He frequently speaks of this.

My own specialities
are beginnings and endings.
Everything used to be plausible.

Curl up and enjoy the possible,
draw nearer to the process
which forges the world we live in.

Garner a fair amount of interest.
How much do you need at the present time?
Become the object of your desire.

As the hearse heads home
showers of flowers are thrown.
Time to go in at the deep end.

•

I seem to have lost a language or at least the way to speak it.
Narrative cannot break free from the weight of tradition.
I try to select thematically. A prestigious poet might write a blurb.

I listen but cannot understand. Although classical elements dominate,
they are all based on acute observation of human behaviour
and commercial success. One cannot be too questioning.

The story of revolt proves sophisticated and is never an imposition.
An early piece shows a version of the work of Ludwig Wittgenstein,
whose movements were always logical, his stillness always significant.

Electronic technology creates confusion. Language is
already over the wall and away from where you want it to be,
attempting to fuse rhythm with both structure and abstraction.

Emotion is often conveyed by extreme close-ups,
providing social comment and acknowledging
that artists have to adjust to this new reality.

Far away is close at hand in images of elsewhere.
This was just useless green before I built this,
a long way from the flattering strokes of nostalgia.

The elephants of oppression are always pedants;
it is not language they love, it is the sound of freedom
at four hundred knots per hour, a hundred feet above.

•

The custodians of costume epics and lively debate,
the cardboard cutout of Elvis Costello in the bar,
visitors to the empty park and my bedroom,
metal-bangers with rising economic fortunes,
free vocalists recounting tales of doomed love,
obscure support bands who turn up everywhere –
all responded with singular understatement to
creating within the constraints of materials.

I only just had time to raise my hat
to the counter-pressure of form.
I am determined to cross the hidden lake,
stimulated by the shakiness of self-destruction.
Life is suddenly and exhilaratingly right:
it has a geometrical tightness mirrored
on the other side of the cultural hemisphere.
It remains legitimate to write with political directness.

The rest of the industry remains unconvinced,
keeping an eye on the not-always-honest magicians
who have learnt to circulate their work
through brightly-coloured magazines,
attempting to shape a future outside of context.
Where did they come from, where are they going,
these literary nomads recycling scraps of discourse,
who hardly know themselves what they have made?

Language apparently antithetical to nonsense,
genuine emotion unmatched by the victim's testimony,
page-long footnotes in passages of autobiography,
grotesque parables of illusion and disillusion –
all this they try to reclaim as heroic mythology.
Names undergo several cryptic transformations;
they inflate the traditional ideas of their period,
reinforce tendencies recorded in scholarship.

Seemingly obscure imagery can unite conflicting energies.
Fluency flows through words to the engine house,
leading to quotation and many notes of apology.
In a letter printed about this same issue, objections:
'Take me for a hard-boiled unimaginative poetic reader
and a large international movement, but grand passions
cause problems later, and have one serious disadvantage –
the result is a breathless paraphrase of the same thing.'

The tears are falling down my cheeks as I tell you this.
I sit in my study, speechless, recognizing nobody.
Appropriately enough, emotions shatter into fragments.
Style functions less as a symbol of transcendental striving
than as a procedure which informs broader patterns –
all the expected incidents, sayings and anecdotes are incorporated.
I do not feel obliged to justify my practices in manifestos;
nothing can happen without the future being announced.

WONDERS OF ANIMAL LIFE

I. HERDS, PACKS AND COLONIES

There are many things
beyond the region
of our understanding:

the optimist,
the bully,
society's victims,

the professional thief,
the ne'er-do-well,
even the altruist.

The children
of the wilderness
shivered for ages.

Man's knowledge of difference
may be described as prolific
and shown to be fairytales,
certainly as wonderful.

Imaginary difficulties
are inaccuracies.
The farthest corners
are being conquered;

climate and civilization
will combine to produce
men of unsleeping energy
and restless ambition.

We are apt to forget
force of habit has made us.
How then does the snake crawl?

We are accustomed to think
of the sea only by night.
It is a very curious thing.

We should attribute progress to
mechanical stresses and strains.
There is a reason for this.

We constantly find, have noted.
We speak. We have evaded
a descent to the dangerous ground.

We must drift with the current.
Intensive effort always produces
structural changes and little power.

More fictions
it is hard to believe.

A whole new nation
is destined to rise –

a little shaky
and ill-defined;

a dense cluster of
workers in conjunction.

Communal life
allied to reason

A pretty idea
but nothing more.

Fact is always
at a distance.

INSTRUCTIONS FOR THE JOURNEY

1.

Burn coffee until the smell hangs in the corner of your room. Try to read while the radio offers up small sounds and burst of noise. Attempt a tightrope walk between possibilities.

Breathe in the bitter aroma, black and sticky in your throat. Listen to new music. Read last year's newspapers, their fading glossy supplements and unengaging book reviews. Aim for isolation and abandonment.

Consume novels you would not otherwise read. Do not bother with the sights proposed by your guide book. Move within the landscape, accumulating detail. Speculate on your past. Possess superficial scraps of detail.

Produce an inventive Postmodern recombination of Modernist components. Go out for a newspaper and at the same time buy a pepper steak. In such fragments can be found the key to the whole enterprise.

Your definition of the aesthetic may be broader, but demand reverence from each viewer. It is an idea of change, dramatic in its own quiet fashion. Tranquil oases and rhythmic inflections articulate the relationships among diverse spaces.

Eastern thought is no less admissible for a Westerner than is European thought. Draw nearer to the process which is the world we live in. Keep everything from the past tucked out of sight.

You are on your way. In this context it is possible to return.

2.

Sit writing at a table. Imagine a clock in a glass case. Read in bed or in a deckchair on the lawn.

Operate entirely outside of discussion. Make plans that are more interesting. Keep the excitement intact.

Make your living from robbing tombs. Accept diverse structures as valid. Become open to all possibilities.

Eliminate social problems. Wipe away centuries of class division, inserting a layer of ironic distance.

Discourage rhetorical activity. Battle against the impotence of the materials at hand. Be rapid, detailed and determined.

Use television more naturally. Incorporate faith into a novel. Recognize the need to speak of God.

Carefully refabricate memory. The past is less fictional than the present.

3.

Reduce your life to a book full of cuttings, photos, mementoes, and one or two watercolours by a lover. A book small enough to carry with you everywhere.

When you are in the dark, swim toward the light. Do not be afraid. Remember a promise you once made.

Trace a finger in the dust, shake the sand from your shoes. Turn and meet the day.

Know that the morning is coming. Smile in the dark while you wait for the dawn.

Converse with strangers and do not despise your differences. Let the people you find yourself with be simply who they are.

Sing in the dusk, pray in the morning. Stay silent and accompany the one who always needs to speak on their journey.

If you are in the dark, sing about the light. Do not be afraid, you will remember nothing except a promise you once made.

Leave your life behind like a book, pages fluttering in the breeze. Breathe in the sunlight and walk among trees.

Let your life become dust. Turn and face the light.

Let me tell you something of what I mean about
the distinction between making and creating.

Sometimes consistency is equated with sincerity –
it may not necessarily be the same thing.

Connect yourself to your own sources and systems;
communication will increase the reach and range.

Technology creates the confusion of the present day
the failure to find a particular type of certainty.

There's no interference here, but no assistance either;
experience is the mark of individuation and of particularity.

Our sense of continuity is flagging a bit
as we push aside artists that have had their moments.

I know how much everyone wants to discover –
everybody is struggling to find their own style.

I just jot things on scraps of paper and lose them,
cultivating the extremes, wrestling with inability.

I practise my own kind of transcendentalism,
leave space in the fast lane for others to pass.

•

It seemed very fashionable at one time,
the kind of energy given off by hysteria;
another form that the form you're making can take…
Both come from the hands of the same creator.

I don't pretend to end up with a new language –
I refuse to do that. It's my social upbringing.
Can you envisage some convergence between music and art
relying on human resources and available technology?

There will be an orchestra; illustration has to come into it.
Because I want to include noise in a musical work
there is occasional repetitiveness and evocation of tension,
lukewarm beats emerging from improvisation…

Does it get better from anyone else's point of view?
The reactions to my music are predictable;
colossal ignorance is no surprise to me.
Keep on eating until you're finished,

re-establish a taste before it becomes decadent.
It may surprise you that my wok is full of blood,
but there's clearly nothing to arouse suspicion.
Screams come from the direction of my kitchen.

•

Conceptual matters will concern us:
an endless line of candles along the tideline,
yellow flashes blossoming from his collar
(explained by the absence of electric current).
All instruments agree it is an extremely cold day.

The solution is the interpretation of public space,
the metaphysics of nomadism, mystery religions,
traced out in the movement of grand narratives
along a broken line of zigzag flight.
A change in direction might salvage a career.

History gives us cause for flexibility and adventure.
There is an enormous amount of trash in this room;
a need for stability and order in the flow of events.
Scrawled translations prove discussion took place –
I end up letting myself be convinced.

•

Talk about potency – my memory has blurred!
(One of the reasons I don't like abstraction.)
I keep fumbling with new interpretations,
find ways through telling silences and irony,
fine tune the verbal to an absolute minimum.

An artist may radically deceive himself,
simply long for new inspiration, explore
the operation of unnatural sounds upon the mind;
apparitions may make him question
his ability to make memorable phrases.

All perception is relative:
images often suggest an essence beyond
with their evidence of distortion.
I have found that things come nearer that way,
are brought to life, stir the imagination.

It's a self-refining process which takes for granted
that meaning exists and, if you press the point,
will form the basis of an equation for anything else.
A kind of cultural fulfilment drives the answerer
to exhaust his dictionary; a fine addiction.

The customs that have the most meaning
may be those that are most universal.
Painting is an old man's occupation.
We were once good friends but now
we don't see each other any more.

•

I gave him everything he wanted at the time:
a small regular income for the family to rely on,
a basic format of redemptive utopias,
a certain kind of preconscious feeling.

Mounted shock combat was not his business,
he felt obliged to oppose sacred order.
He was gripped by desire from behind,
and when it was time to get off, he got off.

It was difficult to have any relationship
lost in a labyrinth of back streets.
There was an emergence of feeling;
he knew there could be no silence.

Relativism is in no way easy to define...
colour can take over the function of form,
drama become ritual, a lyricism of waste;
relationships are as haphazard as a pile of laundry.

Those first, subversive stabs of angina,
the short cut through the woods to town,
the manifest incapacity of machines to deliver,
cause a gradual change in the nature of existence.

Mannerism sabotages reality, becomes
a story to pass from one generation to the next.
I keep brailling these mouldings,
translating them into shrewd evasions.

I am reinventing hermeticism for myself.
I loathe all popular culture,
like to think of myself as a gardener
as a voice once again overtakes the wind:

'It may surprise you but my work is full of love.'

POLAROID EPIPHANIES

for Andy Brown, who helped

> 'Music is the arithmetic of sound
> as optics is the geometry of light.'
>   – Claude Debussy, quoted on a beermat.

This is no other place.
Waken into light beyond
what I can see or make.
Turn to face this light.

A child's ambition is to
be old. A single error.
In love with their lives,
the stars are dead.

Renegade, drum you down
a diversion of stars.
It is with these we must
take the stationary voyage.

•

A fan, a laser mirror,
a decibel, a muslin sheet.
A few words arranged side by side.

Another experiment all done with dots:
as early as fateful summer
atoms suddenly give back the light.

•

A spectacular display of colour
produced the atmosphere,
the lights beautiful to look at
but deadly to the traveller.

Spraycan bandits on silent wings
spread all over the planet.
By evening there was fighting
in the outskirts of the city.

We sneaked in through the back door,
feeling the need to make connections.
At half-time the brothers slipped out,
smoking fervently in the open doorway.

Nothing to do, so ten minutes later we left.
The abiding question: how to disfigure the world?
Conversation not limited to time or space
we play down the pain of entering language.

•

Either not very important
or subject to authority,
everything becomes
predestined to wander.

Fostered by sunlight
a powerful electric spark
just happens to be
controlled by impossibility.

What you might call myth
is contradicted by the facts:
all these reactions identical,
every jot and tittle.

•

Contrary to general belief,
Man was a reality at last,
employed to play atmospheric music.

Curiously enough,
for all his enterprise,
the soundtrack came to a halt.

Contradictions apart,
silence made it easier to compose:
noise was a solution, not a problem.

Contrasting with this,
more and more people seemed to be
heading towards structure and form.

Contingency dictates
opposition between order and disorder.
We aren't the ones allowed to celebrate.

•

I'm dealing with a creator that failed.
You get his number and he'll give you mine.
Everything works better than it used to,
it is our manner of thinking that is so simple...
but we have produced some extraordinary things.

The photographs and sleevenotes
paint a vivid picture of instruments
used deliberately to vibrate cold air.
Like the smell of hospitals in winter
the sound fills everyone with dread.

You know everything they think is wrong!
Live sounds have a different quality,
expressing the situation as a whole.
Illumine and transform and elevate the consciousness –
all of our lives could become music!

•

I have it figured
on crease-eyed paper:
books on the shelves
and all the world outside.

A person with nothing
inside grows afraid.
You want to be surprised?
Imagine more life

struggling for freedom
inside the glass jar;
the loneliness of the ocean
and the discoloured world.

The Museum of Light
for Bob Garlitz

In search of the ghost of punk; the ecstatic moment,
however minimal; swept up in its incoherence,
I embrace history and try to make it open up.
The fashions of the day scare me as much as anyone.

If there's one thing more worrying than a survivor
it's a group of them organised into a network;
the preposterous seriousness of these pedants.
Mass rhetoric continues to be a plausible proposition.

Heroes are uneconomic, with no claims to power.
It isn't simply a question of taking up old tools
and making towering projections of the human spirit,
there must be a shared ground or area of dialogue.

The extremism I once sought has been edited out.
Having perfected this stance, an exquisite anguish,
I chose epiphany over faith, with a shudder of denial
and a declaration that I would not repeat old mistakes.

Activity takes the form of interpretation and judgement;
I bring up the rear with indeterminable precision.
In such cases my work is merely show, a performance,
an act of surrender as liberating as any act of control.

I want to give up the ghost and be enthralled,
am very much concerned with my own plight;
take full credit for taking conceit on board.
I have no desire ever to lurch into lucidity.

•

Making something implies process as well as object.
Now I can balance I never tire of the familiar,
would enjoy very much seeing what *you* do with it.
I want to introduce you to voices other than your own.

I like an alluring, oratory voice which is
all the better for discussion and hybridisation.
The question of fusion becomes much clearer
in the light of changing practice.

There are always questions about systems.
Do you want self-revealing process or not?
The poem does not need its own citations,
otherwise it will never surprise you.

Do you know the source of the quotation?
Does it bother you? Have you been keeping quiet?
We experience the otherwise, as well as
fictional paradoxes, within the centre.

Sometimes you will hear a prohibiting voice,
feel overwhelmed. However irrational,
you won't be able to recall the flux of events,
or remember if time is a flow or an inner veil.

I'm not sure whether I've seen the prints, wonder
if painting benefits from walking away from it?
There's a big mass of stuff to get one's hands on,
begin to plunder. I hate overblown nostalgia.

•

Suddenly a racket coming from far away
penetrates the surroundings. Presences advance.
Nothing can stop this moment of delight,

these cascading layers of musical expression.
I recognize the process itself – how after a while
a formation returns as though never departed.

With enfolding radiance and affirmation
the music is never less than lovely,
verging on white noise and violent hysteria.

Sound no longer conforms to the norms.
The song becomes a real-time situation,
a delirious out-of-control rollercoaster.

Experience has been installed as something
pretty much out there in the world,
received imagery. Maybe I am just tired,

but I find hardcore drum'n'bass unlistenable,
know little about visceral versions; am constantly
aware that this is a reaction against sophistication.

If noise is the point at which language buckles
and life shatters into fragments, then we must
listen to these prophets of escalating discontent.

Time has no more importance than any other concept.
The creative process is a magpie with shifting eyes,
whose letters home are one of the joys of my life.

•

My search is for a more credible seriousness.
It is about words in the most elastic sense,
a different kind of trance experience,
an attempt to articulate communal space.

The darkness hasn't necessarily gone
but now I am finding my way unaccompanied.
Apocalypse and repetition, consumer leisure culture
are all different routes to oblivion.

I know the existence of the world,
the social constitution of reality,
but what if the natives are hostile
and see everything differently?

I've always had a very negative feeling about
sermons and speeches, the effect of clarity.
I need to redefine what is usually meant
by the transmission of images, need a break:

a good weekend drifting, winging it north;
deep and bottomless floods over the land,
a clarity and array of images, space...
My friend points up into the still blue air:

'I have put the moon into this museum of light.'

•

I move on, head towards summer,
tear out of orbit, the changing lines of light;
so lovely flying full steam ahead...
Who guards the regions of hope?

Keep scribbling in some meaningful way –
I am always intrigued by your amendments.
Don't worry about sending more money,
just keep the damage within boundaries.

I question the apparent solidity of walls,
the dryness of long prosaic sentences,
paying for a studio I do not use very much.
We have different tastes, or so it seems.

Let's follow the path between the two,
allowing form to filter forward and back,
keeping it in the dense jungle of words.
I offer you the bowl of my heart.

FURTHER INSTRUCTIONS FOR THE JOURNEY
(Know your place)

1.

Describe the heavens according to tidal changes, sunset and sunrise. Interpret signs as warnings, fantastic specimens of the ruins of modern times.

Stop to marvel at the feelings experienced by people who explore the past. What turns up here fascinates. Greatness today is constituted by a crowd of spectators.

Experience the same anger as others, using poorly scripted dialogue. Be impulsive and nocturnal, aware of the chance interventions of industrial sounds.

Accompany the dead down below. Steer toward the island, destroy all the magic. Impose silence and submit to the uncanniness. Souls are frightened of noise.

Ignore the liquid polyphony of traffic, the permanent daylight. Let the flash of a furnace on the hill, the glow of a thousand windows, all lighted, be your tonal centre.

Imagine a future so simple what is imagined is possible, a new life lived as sublime moments of joy. Write the manifesto for this evolution.

Dream of pursuing utopia. Adopt strategies of beauty.

2.

Walk by the lost generation and ask difficult questions. Ask what has happened, smile and look at the sky. Prophesy an encounter with wisdom.

Look at somebody looking at someone else. Imagine them arguing, frolic with words and their senses. Grumble about having to wait.

Create dense harmonic dissonance and allow it to subside. Sit at home and write masterworks. Study the original gravity information.

Take hold of the system and reverse it. Undertake a radical critique of society, swapping entertainment for emotional aerobics. Rewatch a favourite film.

Plagiarise your own thesis. Set up a digital archaeology which can take the place of native intelligence. Deny all subconscious links.

Sell several valuable books at the same time. Pile memories up against the wall and invite shame into the living room. Run away from yourself.

Fly by night. Ignore the groan of thunder, fling clouds across the sky. Eat rice and cabbage. Call for more champagne.

Consider the blood on your fingers. There is nothing to know.

3.

Create imaginary kingdoms in places you do not know. Be lost in the territory you invent. Sigh at the fading of stars.

Choose your place in the team. Travel as the vanguard of something new, detached from the power of your past.

Make place a portal to memory, a potent brew of autobiographical fragments. Away from the city and past that you love be levelheaded when melancholic.

See the future as a dressing-up box, a place to belong, like the longhouse or boathouse, the ship or the mooring you glimpse from the train and desire.

Design an imaginary part of England as a pastoral utopia, a fiction. Let open fields and the river, a coal fire, compete with the pavement for your heart.

Know your place. Nothing is or ever was sacred.

I persuaded the caretaker to admit me.
He'd returned from a long and tiring journey,
wheezed every time he drew breath,
yet kept alive notions of the cosmos,
rejecting earlier proposals to delete copyright
and use instruments in unmusical ways.

I had forgotten to replace the biscuits in the jar.
Like an occupied city whose liberators are near,
I refused to be stuck on the horns of ethical dilemma.
I had to bring back the dead – but nothing's that simple.
I was in no position to predict consequences,
didn't feel it was right to make assumptions.

Two strategies became most apparent:
climb the tree and whistle like a nightingale
or leave the audience out in the cold.
Passive culture flagged down another car,
polished her sunglasses and spoke in rapid bursts.
Our meeting was something of a reunion.

As soon as you suppress the level of debate
you tend toward the desires of the individual.
Having a voice can be taken for granted...
Illusion is all the more gratifying
when the whole thing comes from chance.
Were there really microphones in the room?

I thought he was taking his time on this one.
He'd be standing up there when he wasn't,
may have had a hand in changing things for the better.
There are probably ten billion people on the planet –
what holds them together is not only their shared skills
but the most amorphous and unmelodic of tunes.

Do they deconstruct cultural barriers that inhibit?
Do they separate instruments from the notion of pitch?
Are they true to themselves, the whole question of evolution?
I witnessed a miracle but am unable to report it.
I have no idea how to reconcile the times, or stop the pain;
have surrendered my life to you and receive nothing in return.

•

Here I am sitting in a little room
creating a climate in which flowers grow.
I have the urge to scatter all my photographs.

I am indifferent to the question of truth,
interminable lists of rules and exceptions
and dinners that consist of nothing but chillies.

Such things can only bring about destruction,
raise up the worst aspects of human beingness.
I do not murder and deceive and bully all the time.

Strangers sometimes cross my path;
light individually defines each of them.
Questions of self-indulgence loom large.

I wonder about matters of body language;
but there may be some lingering irony
travelling in the same regions as me.

•

The preamble needs to be edited:
I might say this today and tomorrow
something entirely different.

The detective doesn't seem to like this.
He hopes there will not be a revolution,
thinks he will wake up as somebody else.

He knows it is difficult to monitor resistance,
for the world is an endless dance of particles.
He stands outside my apartment,

miming a more flexible attitude to rigidity;
but misinterpretations are never innocent.
The sand saps his energy and creeps into his shoes.

Around the curve of the dark corridor
the gossips of the house sit on a bench,
all dressed in bright robes and headgear.

Sometimes only a single word has meaning
as everything flows towards him.
He has passed the boundary of light.

•

The owner of the nightclub spelt it out:
music still too new to be named or defined;
a state of emotional exhaustion;
an austere sanctuary of light and shade.

One of the wildest drummers in the world
improvised in overdetermined ways.
He ran his fingers across a big lump of coal,
phrasing the beat. The electric did not work.

A wind started up. Long mellow notes followed,
almost forming recognizable shapes,
modest in scale and well-constructed.
Restlessness had no effect on his performance.

The five musicians who remained rented a room
and from time to time undertook interviews,
refusing politely to answer any questions.
This mysterious personal charm is creativity.

•

There is so much literature to choose from –
I fail to think of a single compelling reason
not to plunder the ruins of culture;
what I appropriate is not inspiration.

Instead of argument I use sarcasm,
present everything with mystifying banality.
I am truly gifted and doing something unspeakable;
am uplifted through the sheer joy of creation.

How can you miss the music, magically alive?
When can we meet? I have something to tell you.
You do not have to read all these pamphlets;
there is no more need for shared experience.

I saw you crawl into language's vehicle,
determined to discuss ideas and possibilities.
Temperature and humidity were moderate;
a bottle was opened and passed around.

Words cannot be damaged; we know their basic story –
how they make themselves at home, refuse to install order.
I hesitated to invite them up, wrongly so as it happens.
It was a delightful visit, and they would like to meet you.

THE STANDING STILL OF THE PRESENT TIME
Seven Sermons For The Dead

No more discourse. The impossible is already done:
the diagrams made actual, the decision understood,
achieved with the same precision others arrive at
only when faced with the experience of death.

Everything changes. We watch with excitement
a cinema of gestures, not relying on dreams.
Sampling the memory of something *other*
which can never be cancelled out.

•

Watching history evaporate in disorganization,
the little cable-cars still climbing the steep streets,
I believe we must not leave everything to chance.

If you are lost in the jungle you must always try and find a river.
We commute between the garden and these muddy waters,
drawn by fire and music to the slow shifting current.

The heart's enlargement is the blindness of non-feeling.
At the centre a group of decadent and bored victims of the times
intent on rendering the paradise myth irrational,

who imagine themselves to be composing processes,
but end up only with shattered objects. Where is
the serpent lurking? The madman alone is calm.

•

Repeating the work he has already done
chaos crouches at death's window,
waiting for the receptionist to announce him.

He doesn't tell stories, they tell him.
The audience is distanced,
we are separated from each other.

Close-ups intercut with long shots.
Dull inflected tones spike you,
picking out a pulse to suit the hidden being within.

The moon is a guide through future reverie,
laden with notions associated with belief,
urban sensual pleasures lost and excluded by all.

The final shot is freeze-frame,
sight and sound are muted.
Visions punctuate the starfield,

lightning strikes the high pylon.
Here is the mystical kiss of God;
we are all entirely one being.

•

Nothing seems miraculous in this room;
it is the space of those who move through dreams.

Death to me is purely a human idea.
We are already in stasis,

changing and continuing to change;
aching for the images we cannot bear –

the colour of the spirit invisible by nature,
our isolated reflections inheriting the dark.

Mine is the space of absolutely anywhere.
Nothing seems miraculous. This is the room.

•

The festivities lasted for several days,
the sombre monastery ablaze with lights.
They drummed up a good head of steam
and tried to convince me you were dead.

I laid my gifts nearby and rowed away,
refusing to take part in their games,
wanting again the answers I cannot hear,
not having the speed to form questions.

I don't know whether they imagined me
or created me. The dejection deepens.
Mine is the space of those who move on,
lost and excluded by all. It will make a good story.

•

Bathed in red above desolate docks,
the heavens were still and cold.

The rain had finished and the sky was clearing,
the evening sun splintered in the high tree.

We only see images in light, subliminal colouring.
We can only experience through reading and the imagination.

Go get the books out of storage.
Gather up the force that is in things and put it to good use.

The unconscious senses are operating all the time,
carrying the invisible, the past and other subtle bodies.

Non-visual intuition changed the pattern
of the waves of the sea behind him.

The procession stretched over nautical miles,
bleached into a sunset which came from under water.

Transferring to the sky, we drank in our reflections.
We rediscovered the night, the needlepoint of stars.

I do not understand obsession
or the sweet mystery of pain,

but we landed like a dream,
with a barking howl of joy.

See what has become:
the sea; a ship; fire, flowering in the sky.

•

I rode my horse
into the land of grief.

Gravity was with me.
The stars were splashed with blood.

I loved him
but could not go with him.

I long for paradise,
endless and blue, unknown.

I give my creased self up
to the awful future,

watch the snow falling,
the landscape in a coal fire.

There is no reason
to move from where I am now.

We are swimming in grace.
We are full of the light.

What a marvellous swirl of meaning and nonsense!
I've got the noise and a clear intention to riff out,
love how the pleasures of each line circle around
and get recaptured later as a whole.

I will have to write special commentaries
on the sections that are my own work.
I am curious to see the final presentation
and how it will continue to unfold.

Every changing shape and phrase
does not appear the least out of order.
You want to talk about meaning?
I found a couple of clues a while back.

Go on, hit me in the head with a shovel –
that's the kind of criticism I understand.
Let me show you a page from my notebook,
the psychic snag and pull of unrelated images.

I remember the day that snapshot was taken,
recall what I have told you about the place.
I wrote every morning to establish a pattern,
lost patience with the conventions of the craft.

Any piece of information is potentially mine;
I am moved by the wish to preserve something.
I nearly always have a specific mission
when I insert myself into the work this way.

No more secret rules or liberal indignation –
I have performed the last few days as usual.
Now you change the topic of conversation;
I am grateful for your timely intervention.

•

I like the idea of being inside your brain and looking out,
cutting-up the printed word, scrutinising the bus timetable,
overseeing the widespread destruction of little magazines.

This is the challenge: to go back and become the caretaker,
step delicately through the plaintive wailing
and remind the poet of his or her own mortality.

The avant-garde community remains fogged and flawed,
torn on one side, a meeting point for intellectuals
who find themselves at war with themselves.

Free cinema provides valuable experience.
Splintered moments seem casually deployed –
there is no point in a certain course of action.

Prize money is offered to maintain the attack;
a chilling speech given to the men in the guardhouse.
The quartet seem to have grown to the power of ten.

There are enough gestures without plot going on.
The pulse of pleasure has a voice and a big backbeat,
is carried forward by the energy change produces,

envelops any spectators with dogged thoroughness,
reminding them of past traditional values,
sharing their suspicion of the metropolis.

•

It was the dregs of summer. The city
was loud with beer-fuelled conversation.

We heard yelling and then a terrific noise;
a police car stopped out on the street.

I kept my door locked, my head down.
After all, it was your dream, not mine.

Maybe the concert was a set-up job?
It contained some rather strange sounds...

For a pianist his style was quite different,
could have been subject to more self-editing.

The audience cranked the handle, made a roar.
Instruments hummed and whirred, then sang.

Outside the window not-yet existent music
hovered over the ochre-ripple of the desert;

a drop of hot asphalt dripped down the sky;
at sunset the water glistened for our ritual.

Living and inanimate things were all transformed;
I had a difficult time remembering where I was.

Before my thoughts went from nice to now
I listened to that kind of stuff alone in my room.

•

As soon as it had ended
I gathered up the possessions
I needed for my journey.

The city is always five miles
from the edge of the world,
from where I want to be.

The rain began during the night.
I certainly enjoyed it, it conjured
up real excitement as I slept.

Setting aside my paintbrush
I put on my robes, plunged
into actualisations of myth.

The river was dark as oil;
the streets looked fantastic;
the revs in my engine went up.

I drifted further into the cave.
Silence echoed within the silence,
an imaginary low-pitched hum...

•

Industrial sound and hypnotic drones –
I like these two things to go hand in hand,
frequently find them tangling with the soprano,
catch glimpses of a secret but continuing ritual.

Barbed wire rolls on the neighbour's garage roof;
smears and scrapes; a ghostly light in the gallery;
something growling at the door of the white room –
performance should be the raising of the dead.

Headaches and noise; a crime that never happened.
Too much to listen to, and nothing to paint–
a formal arrangement, flat areas of colour
with little possibility of emotional range.

Art should have the power of the military;
a rebel army, expecting to be attacked.
Assumptions like this are hard to test –
the prosection can find no reliable witnesses.

Hippocrates, Father of Medicine,
paused for what seemed like an age.
He appeared incredibly old.
He was born on the island of Cos,
was visited by the philosopher Plato,
was the first man to describe clearly
and concisely; was, indeed, an *observer*.
He was also the first to systematically note
(always referring to it as his Art)
the effects of work, exercise, food
(herbs like rosemary, mint, thyme and parsley),
weather (high winds) and climate
(jagged particles of ice and snow).
He died at the age of one hundred.

Houdini the escapologist
(how could such a skinny lad
keep such a big man above water?)
was naturally intrigued.
He was born in Pennsylvania
and took an interest in ornithology.
His tall figure and reddish-brown hair
would arouse terror in millions.
His ambushes were always
too clever for his enemies
(had they watched a little longer
they would have raised the alarm).
He was a man of wit, too,
although his outspoken bluntness
rebounded on his own head
when he branded Cook a liar.
Returning to Greenland
(his opportunity came),
he estimated that he must
have passed over the very spot
about which the Earth revolves.
(how they find their way there
is something still not worked out).
Eskimos greeted him with joy.

Helen travelled alone all over America.
Incredibly, she had by then become
an accomplished horse-rider, swimmer,
yachtsman, dancer and trick cyclist
(it was intended to be crewed by three people).
In the meantime Major Dobbin (in a fashion
typical of his kind in the early part of the century)
had heard that Amelia 'intended to marry' (her words)
the hairy Siberian who Shackleton had introduced
(it was expressly requested) to this creator.
It was the chance James had been waiting for –
indeed perhaps this started his anatomical investigations.
In turn Constantine was determined
(if a way could be found) to harness the Rajah.
In other words to extend the Empire –
the most dangerous sport in the world.
It was a good plan, the fastest defeat in history
(it could hardly have been otherwise).
Evans succumbed first in the conflict,
immediately receiving a mortal wound
(it was the end of the road for him).

They didn't know what they were doing. Men
(having all the faults of the worst petty official)
have never shown such endurance at any other time.

FINAL INSTRUCTIONS FOR THE JOURNEY
(Pilgrimage)

1.

Walk in the morning with a great display of unspoken words, oblivious to what you wanted to see in the first place.

Collaborate with leading figures. Learn to control excitements and panic. Be dependent on people, not books.

Make convincing decisions. Imagine streets with a lot of people. Forget the difference between televised events and reality.

Match the intensity and savagery of gossip with collective creation. Agitate for peace. Literary strategy is as risky as military strategy.

Let the world sing to itself. You have an obligation to keep your dreams worthwhile; the effects you desire require time.

Fate is not the same for all: as you can see, the door is closed.

2.

Choose one of the paths in front of you. Put the car gently into gear and drive off. Arrive at a natural diction.

Hesitate before crossing the bridge. Scan the incredible landscape. Repeat the manoeuvre in its entirety.

Reduce your story to its aphoristic rudiments. Mispronounce one word. Reach beyond yourself towards Utopia.

Prepare placards with the names of the dead on. Guide souls through the kingdom of shadows. Bathe in the icy blue wind.

Create a permanent residency for success. Stop speaking to yourself: poetry is less and less wanted in our society.

Did I hear lightning or see thunder? It was raining on the other landscapes too.

3.

Disguise propaganda as education. Interrupt whoever is speaking, entering into their fictional situation.

Emphasize the precariousness of the institution. Reorganize networks. Soar above the orchestra and chorus.

Wait for the delayed miracle. Cease to be coherent. Push things too far and try to contradict the small print.

Prove your docility. Stake out part of the promised land and share the hallucination. Shut yourself in your room and scream.

Warm yourself in the blaze of noon. Live in an animated universe. Don't pretend to be building a cathedral.

Try to understand everything. Language is remarkably persistent.

SOURCES

In places, the poems in this collection draw on the following material:
Content's Dream by Charles Bernstein;
Bloodaxe Books' *The Catalogue;*
private correspondence from Andy Brown, partly published
in *Acumen* magazine as 'From a Correspondence';
Silence, For The Birds and *Empty Words* by John Cage;
various writings of Gilles Deleuze;
The Last Thing He Wanted by Joan Didion;
Shooting Elvis by R. M. Everz;
private correspondence and poems by Robert Garlitz;
Architecture After Modernism by Diane Ghirado;
Port Tropique by Barry Gifford;
Natural Grace by Rupert Sheldrake & Matthew Fox;
Derek Jarman, Dreams Of England by Michael O'Pray;
The Black Goddess by Peter Redgrove;
Blissed Out by Simon Reynolds;
The Matter Of The Heart by Nicholas Royle;
Scratch magazine No. 17;
White Chapell, Scarlet Tracings, Lud Heat, Suicide Bridge and
Lights Out For The Territory by Iain Sinclair;
Space Is The Place by John Szwed;
Ocean Of Sound by David Toop;
World of Wonder magazine Nos.1-200

RUPERT M. LOYDELL is a prolific writer, his work having appeared in magazines worldwide, in anthologies and in several solo collections. He has read his poetry at many literary festivals and events around the UK, and in the United States. He is Managing Editor of Stride Publications, and Visiting Fellow of Poetry at Warwick University.